BOA
EDITIONS
LIMITED

Red Suitcase

poems

Naomi Shihab Nye

BOA Editions, Ltd.   Brockport, New York
1994

LC #: 94-78069
ISBN: 1-880238-14-4 Cloth
ISBN: 1-880238-15-2 Paper

First Edition
94 95 96 97 7 6 5 4 3 2 1

The publication of books by BOA Editions, Ltd., is made possible
with the assistance of grants from the Literature Program of the New
York State Council on the Arts and the Literature Program of the
National Endowment for the Arts, as well as from the Lannan Foun-
dation, the Lila Wallace–Reader's Digest Literary Publishers Mar-
keting Development Program, the Rochester Area Foundation, and
contributions from individual supporters.

Cover Design: Daphne Poulin
Cover Art: Beck Whitehead
Typesetting: The Typeworks
Manufacturing: McNaughton & Gunn, Lithographers
BOA Logo: Mirko

BOA Editions, Ltd.
A. Poulin, Jr., President
92 Park Avenue
Brockport, NY 14420

For my family, and the big family of friends, especially Dorothy, Paula and William, Carol and Amon, Nancy and Lou. And for all the friends who haven't met yet, everywhere.

A person was carrying a very heavy red leather suitcase.
When opened, it contained nothing but a blank sheet of paper.

—Moroccan Folktale

CONTENTS

III. BRUSHING LIVES

TRAVEL ALARM

Because everything still bears
the sweet iron taste of experiment,
a penny pressed to the tongue,
the boy places his mother's
little clock in the broiler.
Way back, down deep,
so she won't see when
she bakes the muffins.

Once she says, What's that smell
in here? Like truck tires
at a car lot—and he grins,
by now having forgotten,
but liking strange odors
that rise in the midst of any day,
strange bells, even the maniac
who kept roaring around their block
till his mother called the police.

Each morning he begs his parents
not to read the newspaper, knowing
how their faces go half-blank
and mad, their hands turn
and turn never finding
the right page.

But the secret woman keeps pitching
the rolled paper into their yard,
the woman called Willie or Freddie,
whom he caught a glimpse of once,
pulling away in her long arrow
of a car.

Later he asks, is it still morning?
If it's noon, why is it so dark?
Some evening when his mother pulls
the broiler wide to find
her melted ring of hours,
now crisp as a wedding collar,
and the two frozen hands,
he'll feel far away,
as if he didn't do anything
leading up to it.

But when she likes the hard new shine
glossing the puckered 3 and
sunken 8, when she says
Now we can never be late

and laughs, and laughs,
the sound of a storm coming
that lifts the air in its path,

when she hands it back to him
and he winds the little key
to hear it ring! Still—
the wild buzz that woke her up
in a hundred different towns—
he'll feel how morning and evening
run together, how bad and good can melt
into something entirely else.

They'll tell his father
when he steps from the darkroom
blinking, they'll say
We have a surprise for you,
and hold it up. It will take him
a long moment even to know
what it was.

Standing together
on the edge of dinnertime
and night, the table half-set
but nothing missing,
no one wishing for any
impossible season,
—when I was smaller,
when you'll be older—
even the trees outside
that should be thinking autumn now
still lit by an endless minute
of green.

*

I

In Every Language

FROM HERE TO THERE

Everything needs readiness,
baskets emptied,
gladiolus spear placed in
a glass.

Before you begin,
before you let yourself move
from here to there,
you attend to little things,
a cat's mouth open and crying,
a thin parade of ants
along the sill.

Something in the way we are made
wants order. Wants three pillows
lined across the head of the bed,
wants porches swept and shades raised.

Before we begin. Before we head into
those secret rooms no one else
has cleaned for years,
where memories rest in heaps,
without cabinets,
and have only to be touched lightly
to shine.

*

THE ATTIC AND ITS NAILS

It's hard up there. You dig in a box for whatever the moment requires: sweater, wreath, the other half of the walky-talky, and find twelve things you forgot about which delay the original search, since now that you found them you have to think about them. Do I want to keep this, bring it downstairs? Of course your life feels very different from the life you had when you packed it up there. Maybe your life has another kind of room in it now, maybe it feels more crowded. Maybe you think looking at this old ceramic cup with the pocked white glaze that you made in college would uplift you in the mornings. Your search takes on an urgent ratlike quality as you rip paper out of boxes, shredding and piling it. Probably by now you've stood up too fast and speared your head on one of the nails that holds the roof shingles down. They're lined up all along the rafters, poking through, aimed. Now you have to think about tetanus, rusty nails, the hearty human skull. A little dizzy for awhile, you're too occupied to remember what sent you up into the dark.

ARABIC

(Jordan, 1992)

The man with laughing eyes stopped smiling
to say, "Until you speak Arabic—
—you will not understand pain."

Something to do with the back of the head,
an Arab carries sorrow in the back of the head
that only language cracks, the thrum of stones

weeping, grating hinge on an old metal gate.
"Once you know," he whispered, "you can enter the room
whenever you need to. Music you heard from a distance,

the slapped drum of a stranger's wedding,
wells up inside your skin, inside rain, a thousand
pulsing tongues. You are changed."

Outside, the snow had finally stopped.
In a land where snow rarely falls,
we had felt our days grow white and still.

I thought pain had no tongue. Or every tongue
at once, supreme translator, sieve. I admit my
shame. To live on the brink of Arabic, tugging

its rich threads without understanding
how to weave the rug . . . I have no gift.
The sound, but not the sense.

I kept looking over his shoulder for someone else
to talk to, recalling my dying friend who only scrawled
I can't write. What good would any grammar have been

to her then? I touched his arm, held it hard,
which sometimes you don't do in the Middle East, and said,
I'll work on it, feeling sad

for his good strict heart, but later in the slick street
hailed a taxi by shouting *Pain!* and it stopped
in every language and opened its doors.

*

JERUSALEM

"Let's be the same wound if we must bleed.
Let's fight side by side, even if the enemy
is ourselves: I am yours, you are mine."
—Tommy Olofsson, Sweden

I'm not interested in
who suffered the most.
I'm interested in
people getting over it.

Once when my father was a boy
a stone hit him on the head.
Hair would never grow there.
Our fingers found the tender spot
and its riddle: the boy who has fallen
stands up. A bucket of pears
in his mother's doorway welcomes him home.
The pears are not crying.
Later his friend who threw the stone
says he was aiming at a bird.
And my father starts growing wings.

Each carries a tender spot:
something our lives forgot to give us.
A man builds a house and says,
"I am native now."
A woman speaks to a tree in place
of her son. And olives come.
A child's poem says,
"I don't like wars,
they end up with monuments."
He's painting a bird with wings
wide enough to cover two roofs at once.

Why are we so monumentally slow?
Soldiers stalk a pharmacy:
big guns, little pills.

If you tilt your head just slightly
it's ridiculous.

There's a place in my brain
where hate won't grow.
I touch its riddle: wind, and seeds.
Something pokes us as we sleep.

It's late but everything comes next.

HOLY LAND

Over beds wearing thick homespun cotton
   Sitti the Ageless floated
poking straight pins into sheets
   to line our fevered forms,
"the magic," we called it,
   her crumpling of syllables,
pitching them up and out,
   petals parched by sun,
the names of grace, hope,
   in her graveled grandmother tongue.
She stretched a single sound
   till it became two—
perhaps she could have said
   anything,
the word for peanuts,
   or waterfalls,
and made a prayer.

After telling the doctor "Go home,"
   she rubbed our legs,
pressing into my hand
   someone's lost basketball medal,
"Look at this man reaching for God."
   She who could not leave town
while her lemon tree held fruit,
   nor while it dreamed of fruit.
In a land of priests,
   patriarchs, muezzins,
a woman who couldn't read
   drew lines between our pain
and earth,

stroked our skins
to make them cool,
   our limbs which had already
traveled far beyond her world,
   carrying the click of distances
in the smooth, untroubled soles
   of their shoes.

*

WORDS WHEN WE NEED THEM

Before this early moment,
another, ripe with rain,
the scent of its own full shape.

Each day the rooster
we have never seen
raises the first greeting
and darkness which holds us
in its loose pocket all night
sets us down.

Now we walk,
waking up rooms,
switching on lights.
Into the breath,
wordless but ripe
with all possible words,
messages not yet gathered
or sent.

Morning looms,
more friend than
the best friend.

We could still say.

*

HOW PALESTINIANS KEEP WARM

Choose one word and say it over
and over, till it builds a fire inside your mouth.
Adhafera, the one who holds out, *Alphard*, solitary one,
the stars were named by people like us.
Each night they line up on the long path between worlds.
They nod and blink, no right or wrong
in their yellow eyes. *Dirah*, little house,
unfold your walls and take us in.

My well went dry, my grandfather's grapes
have stopped singing. I stir the coals,
my babies cry. How will I teach them
they belong to the stars?
They build forts of white stone and say, "This is mine."
How will I teach them to love *Mizar*, veil, cloak,
to know that behind it an ancient man
is fanning a flame?
He stirs the dark wind of our breath.
He says the veil will rise
till they see us shining, spreading like embers
on the blessed hills.

Well, I made that up. I'm not so sure about *Mizar*.
But I know we need to keep warm here on earth
and when your shawl is as thin as mine is, you tell stories.

*

LATE

Your street was named for berries.
We dug and dug in heaps of leaves.
The door to your basement
would never stay closed.
Uncle said to push it till it clicked.
"Come eat!" you'd call,
planting yourself by the table.
We came in with twigs in our hair.

At the bottom of those stairs
was a tomb where old sofas went
and milk bottles grew spider nests.
We stayed outside till the light shrank
into its last deep moment of staring
and the moon came up, a giant other eye.

One night we fooled you,
hiding under the bush,
the yard a held breath.
Your voice trilled for us,
rose higher on its ladder
till it was not calling us at all,
it was reaching for everything you dreamed
that never happened,
years flying out of your skin,
the shadowy baby who wouldn't be born.

We entered sheepishly, looking at our feet.
Today I would answer for all those other things.

*

VOICES

I will never taste cantaloupe
without tasting the summers
you peeled for me and placed
face-up on my china breakfast plate.

You wore tightly laced shoes
and smelled like the roses in your yard.
I buried my face in your
soft petaled cheek.

How could I know you carried
a deep well of tears?
I thought grandmas were as calm
as their stoves.
How could I know your voice
had been pushed down hard inside you
like a plug?

You stood back in a crowd.
But your garden flourished and answered
your hands. Sometimes I think of the land
you loved, gone to seed now,
gone to someone else's name,
and I want to walk among silent women
scattering light. Like a debt I owe
my grandma. To lift whatever cloud it is
made them believe speaking is for others.
As once we removed treasures from your
sock drawer and held them one-by-one,
ocean shell, Chinese button, against the sky.

*

WHITE HAIR OVER
THE ROCKY MOUNTAINS

1.

All these days
I've been secretly growing old:
just now the pilot mentioned snow
and I walked to the mirror
at the back of the plane
to find it sprouting
from my own skull.

How long we have lived together
I do not know,
whether a hair starts out pale
and remains so,
or bleaches white when grown—
I cannot ask the stewardess.

2.

How did these people
become so definite?
They order drinks
as if no other drink would do.
I hover between milk
and Scotch, simply because
the man beside me ordered Scotch
in a positive voice.

Below us the ribs of the earth
fan out in perfect spirals.
No one lives in these regions

of rock and sun.
It is a lucky part of the world;
to grow old without buildings
and roadways,
to dissolve quietly
without feeling stunned.

3.

My grandmother had white hair,
she was a dandelion puff
ready to be scattered.
She used to take me downtown
where we could stare at one another
in plate glass windows,
and I saw through her head,
a mass of buses,
young mannequins frozen
toward Hello.

*

ALMOST, NEVER

What would I do
Without you
My seamstress you
With a needle in your mouth
        —Charles Simic, from "Pain"

He says one thing   she says everything else
all my life this small valley pulled stretched
till the earth rips down the middle
Both say You see it like I do don't you?

Every evening grackles swarm the tops of trees
shouting what might be *gather*
over the houses
into the sky's wide ear

        and the rooms hear them
        the child hears them strike his dreams
        someone almost forty hears
        like a birthday pulling him up
        but he pulls back

a season flies out of our hands
He says This year for sure
She says The door is closed
but keeps beating on it
grackles circle the courthouse park
shouting over the fountain
bottles stuffed in sacks
the wavery men

shouting what might be
change your life
I seem to remember being
many more people
loose weave of wind
knotted with cries

TEXAS, THE FIRST TIME

The state was a ream of paper
spread out flat in front of us.
We were writing a long song,
St. Louis to Mexico, but our throats
felt too dry to sing it.

At a silver gas station a man said
tires would grow bubbles and explode.
A car might spin and fly.
"You had a close call."
His voice was a glistening nail.

For ten thin hours I dreamed of flying.
I gripped the handle till my knuckles ached.
At a roadside stop my father threw a Coke bottle
at a fence post. He was mad at us for arguing.
The silence dripped down for miles.

WHAT SHE WAS DOING AT HOME

School was like a ship they
sent you away upon.
—Michael Burkard

The baby was there—unfair.
I knew whatever she was doing
had fluted edges, a cinnamon center.
I knew she placed snipped rounds of waxed paper
between layers of cookies in the tin.

And I was missing it,
missing everything.
As far away as the monkey
in a rocket.

After school, when I tried to swim back
into her day, she had left it already.
She was washing up on the shores of dinner,
wearing a cool rag pressed between her eyes.

SWIMMER, BLESSED SEA

Well, when this head is clean off and its riddance is
enjoyed, what are the likely results for the headless
one, in the light of the past decade's experience?
—D. E. Harding

1.

Once, pregnant women looked at me
as if I had forgotten something.
I wanted to rap my knuckles
against cribs, flannelette bathrobes,
the meanings of names.
They stood on the edge of an ocean,
poised and confident, arms raised.
The rest of us were just getting older.

2.

Now the world echoes with cries of children:
blue shirt, front cash register, he says his name is Ray.
Now I join the federation of those
who entered days tired and could not lie down.
My mother with pony tail and plaid dress
pulling us to the grocery in a wagon—
probably we whined or wished for something,
her arm ached, and for sure it was uphill.
Once, walking home, a milk carton
burst in her arms. Milk streaming—
her pale, pale eyes. I join the shadow
at table or sink, the leaning, lifting self
that answered "Yes?" a million times.

3.

When you lived inside me I was a boat.
Rising, twirling, you steered me
toward the bed for naps.
I rode those days carefully,
seeking smallest waves.

You raised the flag of a new country in my heart
and all its citizens ran out to greet us
when we arrived.

4.

I love you, hymn and hymnal,
battering oar!
An owl lights your room at night.
I want, I need, immediate bloom.

Now grandfathers stoop
at the grocery store,
touching your fat feet
to their foreheads.

To pregnant women I say *Sister*,
to Self I say *Wait*.
Here is the second story,
telling you more.
This door that opened,
this window that cut off my head.

*

HIS SECRET

The field wraps around him.

He takes in his fist the 3-winged grasses,
the stick shaped like a Y.

Filling his bag with fallen petals,
shiny wrappers, husks.

Filling his eyes.

He is welcoming the bent weed,
spinning the hay.

Tying the shoelace
to the stone.

No one answers his questions better
than the split brick he hit
with a hammer.

Above him, a hundred flying birds call out
"Alone!   Alone!   Alone!"

*

At the heart of the apple,
at the heart of the worm.

A boy filled a bottle with water.
He let it sit.
Three days later it held the power
of three days.

*

THE MAN WHOSE VOICE HAS BEEN TAKEN FROM HIS THROAT

remains all supple hands and gesture

skin of language
fusing its finest seam

in fluent light
with a raised finger

dance of lips
each sentence complete

he speaks to the shadow
of leaves

strung tissue paper
snipped into delicate flags

on which side of the conversation
did anyone begin?

wearing two skins
the brilliant question mark of Mexico
stands on its head
like an answer

*

SOMEONE IS STANDING ON THE ROOF
OF THE WORLD

Strange luck lately, you say,
after weathering the worst luck
anyone could name.
For days I light a candle near
your picture: Angels, find this man
and follow him. I snip the last thin sprigs
of mint from the garden and your family
whom I never knew crowds this house
till one day, waiting at a crossing light downtown,
I think I'm you. It gets stranger
being here, amid these tangled histories,
so strange some mornings say,
"This again?" and cover their eyes.
Not exactly what I'd write in
letters of consolation but, brother,
the leaves are going to sleep now,
underfoot they fold their wings.
A nervous squirrel babbles all day
and the newspaper tells how cold it was
a hundred years ago.
We wrap our sweaters tightly.

How strange to go on in your life
when the ground has shifted
and shaken: our friends in Mexico City
do not stop dreaming of the hole.
Who would say, Look up, Have faith,
Someone is standing on the roof of the world?
Not now anyway. Last week a priest
told the children of a murdered woman,

"One thing I am sure of, God hates this."
How busy He must be, blessing and hating,
worrying and loving, as we lug our burdens
toward anywhere to set them down.

This says nothing of burglars,
how busy they must be too,
following each cord to its appliance,
and the names of pawn shops:
FAIR TRADE, DIAMOND, BIG STATE,
waiting with open mouths to gather
what we lose.

I can't separate it anymore.
Stunned faces, cord of love
knotting with grief, sleepless children
obsessed with their mother's floor.
And the day of innocent birds
which began it all! And always does.
Above curtains, slit of sky is lightening,
pure band of light around the room.
A Mexico City milkman pedals carefully,
basket of shapely bottles clinking...
he leaves his bicycle propped against a wall.
Praise a day which needs milk
to get it going, praise beds,
cushions, drainpipes,
the myth of containment which says
our lives are here, with doors
to walk out of, doors
to close behind us, though each night
the floor echoes more deeply,
the roof of stars seems farther away.

*

MY GRANDMOTHER IN THE STARS

It is possible we will not meet again
on earth. To think this fills my throat
with dust. Then there is only the sky
tying the universe together.

Just now the neighbor's horse must be standing
patiently, hoof on stone, waiting for his day
to open. What you think of him,
and the village's one heroic cow,
is the knowledge I wish to gather.
I bow to your rugged feet,
the moth-eaten scarves that knot your hair.

Where we live in the world
is never one place. Our hearts,
those dogged mirrors, keep flashing us
moons before we are ready for them.
You and I on a roof at sunset,
our two languages adrift,
heart saying, Take this home with you,
never again,
and only memory making us rich.

*

II

Living Where We Do

LIVING WHERE WE DO

I like to think of the man under the house
who failed to place a post beneath one corner,

perhaps so he could pass by 20 years later
waving a rag and humming,
to see if the house had fallen in.

When it hadn't, when he found it sitting firm
in the glaze of western light,
I think he reconsidered all that time
on his knees, with jacks and hammers,
the bubble in the level leaning tipsy left,
the undersides of boards.

*

Julia said—Never live
in a place that's new.
She said it could shrink you.

Find a roof and walls that sang
of joining and cracking
before you were born.

Each time something topples,
each time you send out the small cry with
no home, no healing,
an echo will help pick it up.

*

Evenings, the houses inhale,
let go. Each one emitting
a different little cloud;
today they started school again,
today the woman with wings
and crooked hip came home.

*

Consider the smells
absorbed by walls,
garlic, eggplant,
Molly's pork chops next door
drifting into plaster,
the sweet slow cooking of beans.

Each old house with a baby in it
has a secret.

The hundred year old house we slept in
the first year we were married
pretends not to know us.

I don't mind.
I've seen what vines do
to railings.
Even the telephone wire
we talk over
wreathed in floral pink,
and leaves.

The ex-owner left her wedding gifts
sealed in boxes, stuffed
in a shed. Fifty years—the platter,
the rusted juicer, each card
crumbling inside its envelope.

In a creaky trunk, her husband's clothes.

So many good wishes so late—
then we heard he died in the bathroom
by his own hand.

His white woolen socks
rolled into balls.

*

Go away, the house will wait.
All it ever did was wait,
while crisper villages rose and fell.

Strangers drive our neighborhood
on weekends, waving.

"That doesn't look so bad.
Think what you could do to fix it up."

What it could do to fix you up.

Cold floors,
the little seam around windows
letting in weather—
a vine that snaked inside at night
and wrapped around a pillow—

your head, stem of brief blossoms,
its root lodged deep in the ground.

*

IN THAT TIME

The day had its own shape
like a dress pinned up by the shoulders.
The day was sweeping water past the window.

We were going to live in a tree.
We were placing ourselves on a branch
next to the bird with a borrowed voice.

The river wore one glittering eye,
another eye filled with sand.
The river blinked and blinked.
I should have thought of it.

Once a man leaned over the dark hole
of a well and dropped his name down
into the space between top and bottom,
saying, now float. Come back to me smarter.

I will find out where everybody went.
I will break my pencil into two pencils.

We were going to meet for dinner.
At the edge of the forest, the edge of the city.

Once I stood inside an empty schoolhouse
with a fireplace at each end of the long room,
the 1,2,3 still rolling, a small giggle
tucked into the cracks of the wall.

Outside, cows read the slow text of grasses.
Closed their creamy eyes as they ate.
Goodby, goodby. A farmer was selling that place

for 2 thousand dollars. A river
with a gurgling voice. I closed my eyes.
Some small person threw down
his red coat and ran away.

*

ANY NUMBER

Hole in a sock:
this means we are married,
that you had a hole
and I sewed it shut.

In fifth grade the stones
were stuck to cards
and neatly labeled:
dolomite, quartzite, obsidian.

Now the days
burst into flame.
A baby turns yellow for no reason.
Apache tear could have fifty other tales.

Who can see us as we are,
floating decimals on the year's fat page?
Give me a number, any number.
Let me tell you what I love,

white wall, single-striped plate,
then you tell how it goes together,
serpentine, gypsum,
how many years it takes to make a stone.

*

SINCERELY

The envelope, usually white and slim,
bleached as a shell we might press to our ears,
or striped along its flying borders,
sometimes pink, or brown, or puffed,
having traveled that dark space
of slots and chutes and shelves and bags,
having lost faith of finding
either name written on it
ever again, rises out of Mario's hand
into my own. Or I come home
to find it sleeping
in the black box on the slim pole.

And I am rarely equal to it.

We are visited by strangers, saints.
We are visited by the impudent question.

Who holds the knife, the small blade
in a case carved like a fish?

This slicing, this fine rip,
opens a far world, a world apart,
and I try to take it in.

Cranking the creaky door of the heart.

I.

Thank you. The articles about raising children
arrived when my child was being very difficult
and then they vanished. I am certain

they will turn up and he will be
a good boy. In the meantime,
a page describing where one might purchase
Aloha clothing in the capital city of Texas.
Should you have a need. We think of you.

2.

I am sorry I did not answer for so long
but I have been writing to poets in 68 countries
asking to print their poems in the United States.

Yes I am fine. I used to be fine.
What about you?

Each overseas envelope costs 95 cents to mail.

If someone in a far-off country wanted to print your poem
would you say No? Think of the waves and wires
this envelope must cross. The mountains and muddles.

Actually I have had no trouble
with poets, only with translators and publishers,
the great go-betweens. This task has come between me
and everything else I love. Can you be patient?

3.

You say you are leaving the island.
You sound very enthusiastic about leaving the island.
Since I left the island, all I care to think about
is the island.

It must be different for you.
You grew up there.
You wear the colors of the horizon inside your bruise.

You have lived on the cliff so long,
staring off to sea dreaming what lies
on the other side; the big land, the gasp of
rumpled cities, the flush and certainty:
we are what is happening.

May you find it. In the meantime your island
stays lodged inside me, a mint
I turn over and over with my tongue for its endless
flavor.

4.

Thank you for the books you sent which connect
quite specifically to everything I have been thinking of
for the last 12 years.

How did you know this?

We barely met. We barely brushed one another
in the flood of comings-and-goings.

I tried to think of something to send in return
but kept being distracted
by the woolen doll on my desk from Chiapas,
her pigtails tied with pink yarn.

Do you want her? She wears a look of having been
recently startled.

5.

Sometimes a new sister comes forward, or a brother,
and the mouth opens on a hello so long and wide
whole countries live inside it.

Where were you yesterday?

Each corner and tree worth telling.

Now we will have to make letters shaped like kites,
flamboyant tails ripped from rainbow cotton
knotted together, flapping on the huge ache of breeze
that rides between.

*

BREAKING THE FAST

1.

Japanese teacher says:
At first light, rise.
Don't hover between
sleep and waking,
this makes you heavy,
puts a stone inside your heart.

The minute you drift back to shore,
anchor. Breathe.
Remember your deepest name.

2.

Sometimes objects stun me,
bamboo strainer, gray mug,
sitting exactly where
they were left.

They have not slept
or dreamt of lost faces.

I touch them carefully,
saying, tell what you know.

3.

Cup of waves,
strawberry balanced
in a seashell.

In morning the water seems
clear to the bottom.

No fish blocks my view.

VIOLIN

It's been sleeping under the bed
for twenty years.

Once I let it out every day.
Neighbors picked up bits of music
wedged into grass.

I stroked the resiny hairs of bow.
All my tutors, lunatics, but my mother
left us alone.

Sometimes a sonata
broke in the middle—
I stitched it together
slowly, slowly.

Graceful shoulders,
elegant neck—
what do you know now
that you didn't know then?

*

YEAST

Each morning from the dim secrecy
of the school kitchen, that single scent
sweetens the day—rectangles already baking,
legions of bread on long silver trays.
Like history, it won't stop happening.
Bread spreading its succulent flesh
whatever we learn or unlearn
in the room with faded snapping maps.

Once the map flipped up so hard
Greenland caught me on the jaw
and I had to go to the health room.

Lying on the small cot,
closing my eyes under the ice bag,
I could smell the bread better from there.

Sometimes it seemed so obvious.
I should have been a slab of butter,
the knife that cuts, the door
to the oven.

*

CONTINUAL USAGE

"Central School—The Oldest School in
Continual Usage West of the Mississippi"

No wonder we felt weighted walking in those halls. The black-
boards opened up into cloakrooms. Real cloaks once hung on the
hooks where we draped our nylon windbreakers. The cracks in
the tiles, the old-fashioned spines of our books. I loved a por-
celain fountain in the basement, its dependable arching flow.
Thirty years later I would return to find my fountain still tucked
into its niche, gleaming, rich with quiet servitude. I cried for all
those early places we press our lips. We drank and drank. We
shaped our plump names in the corners of pages. We buzzed with
the humming of desks. What I whispered to Douglas still drifts
out in the far stretches of the galaxy—that's what they taught us
in science. Sometimes an echo caught me by the ear, spoken by a
girl who used to sit in my own wooden desk, and I had to put my
pencil down and think of her. It seemed she said, "Yes," but
what else? She was curious. She had not traveled in a car. Some-
times the distance from the teacher to us and back again was so
far I felt closer to that girl who had grown old and died and re-
turned to her classroom to pay a different kind of attention, this
time.

*

ESCAPE

We raised our hands for the honor of leaving the class—to carry a message, a coffee can of soiled brushes to the janitor's sink. One day the door of the janitor's closet banged shut behind us locking us in with the colors red and blue. Karen, the spindly spineless one, gripped my arm. A light bulb dangled on a long cord. Jugs of bleach lined the walls. We called and called, pounding on the door. Red and blue swirled together in a vanishing purple stream. I scrawled HELP! on a paper towel, pressing it out under the crack. But no one passed. If they passed, they didn't look down. By now the class had gone to recess or they would have remembered us. Our empty desks. We held hands. Karen whimpered like a cat. At night the radiators might stop clicking in the building. There would be no heat. We were terrified, but we had what we wanted.

*

SPARROW BONES

He told the secrets of his life
directly into your ear,
you had to stoop way down
to hear him.

He said his stomach had no door.
For years in the fields
he was picking so long in the sun
without a hat on his head
that he hated the things he was picking.
That's why he didn't eat.

His teachers said he paid attention
like a wisp of dust pays attention.
You held out your hand to catch him
but found nothing inside.
His eyes burned, snow on the mountains,
you cannot build a boat from snow.

And he motioned you lower to say
My brother killed a man,
they are looking for me too,
to get even,
my father is dying of a cancer
and then what will we do, what will we do?

He puffed his chest proudly
like a sparrow does after dipping in a puddle
and scribbled his latest address on a scrap of bread bag
before he flew.

*

TONGUE-TIED

Someone just told me our tastebuds die
as we grow older.
They die one-by-one, or in groups.
A child has whole galaxies.
We're lucky by now to retain a few.

This is why a child cries
if something tastes bad.

All day I walk around opening
    and closing my mouth.

The tortilla becomes a deeper tortilla.
The blackberry, packaged in its
    small square crypt,
reaches all the way back to its bush
for me, for what is left of me,
this dissolving kingdom
between my teeth.

*

THE CROSSED-OUT WORD

A letter arrives from New York
advice, criticism

"Be meaner! Tough! Spit it out!
Poems can make us sound too nice!"

He's crossed out a word
near the end of the letter

a word in a crucial location

crossed it out so well I can't tell
a y or a g or even how long the word was

I start imagining all sorts of possibilities

the word was a clue,
now denied me forever

the word, the one thing I could have stood on
a boulder in the landscape

while the rest of the letter
flaps helplessly above my desk

*

LIVING WITH MISTAKES

They won't wear boots.
They march ahead of us
into our rooms, dripping.

Give them a chair.
Where they sit,
the fabric will be wet
for days.
We have to talk about
everything else
in their presence.

*

NIAGARA

Arriving early, before the lovers
have climbed up from their seastruck beds,
she stands where mist can penetrate
the way 7 a. m. changes the world—
softening, quickening little
hopes. She thought the Falls

were out in the country, not in a town.
To be wrong so many times, like finding the pyramids
adjacent to the Cairo bus stop,
or even herself alone in upstate New York
in the middle of a summer when she can imagine
pitching so many things overboard,
not a body in a barrel, not that,
but stacks of manuscripts, yellow stick-um notes,
even what she said yesterday,

into the surging megatons,
the burst of fabulous power that could light our lights
from here to Cincinnati or whatever the loudspeaker shouts
when she rides the boat that dips a herd of slickers
into the blinding white roar, the baptismal boat
where Japanese and Puerto Rican come up equally
wet. Despite the blurred narrative,
she won't forget how she lifted her face into the spray.

Before leaving, she drives around
the Canadian side, entering thrift mart,
dimestore, buying a jug of bilingual bubble bath—

then spins toward the bridge again, refreshed,
sparked by the electricity that accompanies
days marked by nothing but what we see,
as if after all our sober intentions and hard work,
the days that carry us could be these.

*

IN THE PUBLIC SCHOOLS

Her class invents angels
but she won't lift her head.
She is sewing something, gauze suits
for a dead man, I'd guess.
Her fingers crawl, pale radishes
plucked from thin soil.
Her voice oozes toward Lydia,
"You act dumber than you really are."

We know she has children
from the pictures on her desk.
She has a name (spell it right, she drones)
and a paycheck. We don't know what
she wished for that she didn't get.

Each time I enter the room your little mouths open
towards me, desperate drying plants leaning
toward any hose. I would like to pour you full
of rivers, the gallant Mississippi that saved me
when I was small, and stung, or the rich Columbia:
just to see it changes a life. Remind you
of the river San Antonio curling like a sweet vein
through the heart of our town. Even the light
flooding through tall windows igniting chalkdust
becomes something you could dive into,
singing *escape*.

Some days we wad our papers up
and throw them away. Some days, some years.
And the ones who come close but do not love us,
cannot love us, I'd say to let them pass through
painlessly, rivers of dust through a window.
They have nothing to do with you.

*

PROBLEMS WITH THE STORY

The story was too long.

Before you told it, you forgot it.

Before the snake unwound
his infinite body
from around the tree
the head forgot where he was going.

The story had too many beginnings.

If you stepped through a door
twelve others might open.

Did anyone have time?

The story, the story, whose was it?

Did someone else own it too?

The story knotted in the throat of a finch.

Sometimes the story felt cold after you told it.

The story might make his mother nervous.

This was only a translation of the story I heard
through a small crack while sleeping.

This was not the best story.

Angels and bells did not follow this story
but still, I wanted to tell it.

It was the only chance I had
to find you.

VALENTINE FOR ERNEST MANN

You can't order a poem like you order a taco.
Walk up to the counter, say, "I'll take two"
and expect it to be handed back to you
on a shiny plate.

Still, I like your spirit.
Anyone who says, "Here's my address,
write me a poem," deserves something in reply.
So I'll tell a secret instead:
poems hide. In the bottoms of our shoes,
they are sleeping. They are the shadows
drifting across our ceilings the moment
before we wake up. What we have to do
is live in a way that lets us find them.

Once I knew a man who gave his wife
two skunks for a valentine.
He couldn't understand why she was crying.
"I thought they had such beautiful eyes."
And he was serious. He was a serious man
who lived in a serious way. Nothing was ugly
just because the world said so. He really
liked those skunks. So, he re-invented them
as valentines and they became beautiful.
At least, to him. And the poems that had been hiding
in the eyes of skunks for centuries
crawled out and curled up at his feet.

Maybe if we re-invent whatever our lives give us
we find poems. Check your garage, the odd sock
in your drawer, the person you almost like, but not quite.
And let me know.

*

FIREFLIES

Lately I had looked for you everywhere
but only night's smooth stare gazed back.

Some said DDT had cupped your glow
in its sharp mouth and swallowed.
The loneliness of growing up
held small soft pockets you could have filled.

This summer I took my son
to the Texas hills where you startled us at dark,
ancestral droves swirling about our heads.
He thought you held kerosene lamps
the size of splinters. He wanted to borrow one,
just for a second, he said.
My head swooned in the blink of your lives.

Near a cedar-shaded stream where by day
fish rise for crumbled lumps of bread,
you were saving us from futures bereft
of minor lovely things.
You're singing, my boy said that night.
Why are you singing? He opened his hands.
I sang to the quiet rise of joy,
to little light.

*

WHAT IS SUPPOSED TO HAPPEN

When you were small,
we watched you sleeping,
waves of breath
filling your chest.
Sometimes we hid behind
the wall of baby, soft cradle
of baby needs.
I loved carrying you between
my own body and the world.

Now you are sharpening pencils,
entering the forest of
lunch boxes, little desks.
People I never saw before
call out your name
and you wave.

This loss I feel,
this shrinking,
as your field of roses
grows and grows. . . .

Now I understand history.
Now I understand my mother's
ancient eyes.

*

III

Brushing Lives

WHAT BRINGS US OUT

Something about pumpkins caused
the man who had not spoken in three years
to lean forward, cough, open his mouth.
How the room heaved into silence,
his words enormous in that air:
"I won't... be... afraid...
of my... father... anymore."
And what silence followed,
as if each heart had spoken
its most secret terror,
had combed the tangled clump
for the hardest line
and pulled it, intact,
from the mass.

I bless that man forever
for his courage, his voice
which started with one thing
and went to many, opening up and up
to the rim of the world.
So much silence had given him
a wisdom which held us all at bay,
amazed. Sometimes when I see
mountains of pumpkins by the roadside,
or watermelons, a hill of autumn gourds
piled lavishly on crates, I think
perhaps this one, or that, were it to
strike someone right,
this curl of hardened stalk,
this pleated skin...

or, on an old bureau drawer,
the vegetable-like roundness of a glass knob
that the baby turns and turns
emerging, later, from a complicated dream...
the huge navigational face of a radio
which never worked while I was alive
but gave me more to go on than most sounds:
how what brings us out may be
small as that black arrow, swinging
the wide arc, the numbers where silent voices lived,
how fast you had to turn to make it move.

*

LUCIA, YOUR VOICE

From fluent vineyard rolling,
rivers of syllables strumming the air,
I come with you to the garden
where rhubarb shoots its rosy spoke.
We pull and gather,
a shawl of sun on our backs.

Afterwards, the silence is different.
Your voice fills in the cracks
between moment and moment,
sealing them. In the valley
a man is building a house.
Between each block
he spreads the smooth mortar.
People will live here,
sleep here,
safe from the rain.

*

WHAT HAPPENED IN MADISONVILLE

The elegant towered courthouse with four clocks
exploded into flame and burned all night.
Nothing could save it, certainly not
Dickie Bates, who started the fire,
who told the MADISONVILLE METEOR
he wanted to be "a hero in his hometown."

He dropped a cigarette into a box of papers,
thinking he'd be able to put it out.
Firefighters roared in from Huntsville,
North Zulch, Bryan, Campbell.
Bates hadn't liked the way "people looked at him
in town." They looked at him "like he was nobody."
How did they look at him after that?

Judged sane, he went to jail.
Madisonville received the ugliest new courthouse
ever built in Texas. Someone must have talked
them into it; square box, slit windows.
And the elaborate old buildings on each corner
of the square burst into flames, one by one.
Maybe it was contagion, mutual sorrow.
Nobody came forward to say he wanted to be
a hero again.

Girls scooping ice cream under a cardboard model
of the lost courthouse don't remember it.
The woman selling antiques keeps a framed courthouse
picture behind her cash register. "One day
Dickie's parents were in here and some visitor asked me,
—What happened to your old courthouse?—
It was a real bad moment."

The elderly librarian gives the date without pause.
"May 14, 1967. Mother's Day."
As if the sadness has seeped into all their voices.
Bates got out of jail. He's somewhere, age 46.
And the yellowed METEOR shows what the courthouse
looked like, briefly, with that much light inside.

*

FIRST HAWAIIAN BANK

Her hair snipped and tightly curled gives me great comfort, standing behind her in the long line for money. *That someone thinks to do this to hair*, a farmer's neat crop, rows of sorghum with rich furrows between. She wears little turquoise studs in her ears and speaks of her granddaughter with a grandmother's lavish patience. She rides the express bus and tints her lips deep red. *Lives unlike mine*, you save me. I would grow so tired were it not for you.

"IF GOD WON'T TAKE ME, WHY WON'T THE DEVIL?"

Great-great-aunt Leonora, Age 95

We stroke your hands to make you smile,
reduced, reduced. I wish I could help you
die like a present. Carry you over
the threshold, arm around my neck.

You tell me to have more fun.
People just don't have enough of it.
You promise my son each young and beautiful one
will also die. "Think of me then."
He stares, stops cranking the bed.

On your 90th birthday you caught a fish
in Canyon Lake. We'd had a date—
I paced your porch back home,
fearing you dead inside.
Then you drove up grinning wildly,
with the bucket.
"No such luck," you said.
"The fish is dead, not I."

The sky outside your room
washes up blue waves.
We dive into it, released from sour air.
I shake my fist at the sky, loving you,
casting you back.

*

SALT

They have stripped your bed.
The chrysanthemum sheets you died in
have been washed and folded and handed to me
but I could not bring them into my house.
I poured them into the arms of old Mr. Medina
who lives next door and gets water from a pipe
in his yard. "Make curtains," I said.
Somehow your eyes had left the sweetened body
I could not look at in your coffin
and entered his head.

They have parceled out chairs and televisions,
none of which, I am proud to say, came to us.
Long ago we declared our love exempt
from such leavings. Your relatives wrote
their names on masking tape and stuck them
to the underside of every surface they could find.

Each frilly tea rose on your favorite bush
dropped its head the day you died. I stood
in your yard, frozen, swallowing the slow crawl
of sun. You'd taken down the birdhouse
without a hole you hung out "so birds could have
a joke too." I didn't find it funny.
"Well, you're not a bird."

Later I gathered what no one else wanted,
half-empty vitamin bottles, my child's drawings
taped to your wall. "Four Fires Around Flowers,"
he titled one, and I thought of us around your bed,
burning, your shaky hand soothing his hair

and the gravelly whisper, "Beautiful,"
that scared him, it came from
some place so deep.

They stuffed my bag with your honey,
cornmeal, your half-eaten box of crackers,
"low-salt." We ate them in the car.
At the corner of Hackberry Street, Madison said,

"These were the crackers Della liked."
I said, "The very same ones," and felt
the salt welling in my throat, buckets of salt,
the mystery of oceans and our tiny sad world
of drinking glasses, polished, put away.

*

THE SILENCE OF HUTCHINSON, KANSAS:
A LETTER FROM TEXAS

All night the Queen's Crown
unwraps fat heart-shaped leaves,
sticky tendrils curling
in the holes of each screen.
We wake to find it halfway
up the house.

Each day the gray fluted plate
from Hutchinson dries quietly
in the rack. Two women who saved it,
who sold it to me, were selling
the salt shakers of fifty years,
the cowboy, the chef,
the porcelain bride.
They would not smile
for anyone. Later I stood
on the steps of their house
where the sound of fences
and yards rolling forward
held me in its fist.
You stood, and the dog
behind a bush never saw us,
he was sleeping so hard.

I could have said, your life
is here. For years and years
the bricks of your house
had stuck together and people
of your street had gone to work
and come home. It was so silent

each morning after they left
we wore their shoes
from room to room. I could have said,
hold out your hand.

What was it we waited for,
standing on those steps,
pausing at the rim of
so many lives?
Once in the library we lost
each other among the shelves.
I knew you had read every one
of those books and felt terrified
by their spines.

Now I would say how
every song has a blank in it.
I would pause again, to listen.
Envelopes arrive from St. Louis,
Mexico, but never from
the land of wheat.
I would say we said everything
once, long ago, but know it is only
distance welding its shiny crown,
tilting its head.
And the root of silence
which adheres a little deeper each day
is the only thread connecting me
to a town I once entered
and exited by road.

*

SAVED

Once I burned a man's letters
in a metal can in front of him

a wisp of that smoke returns
in the clear breath of mountains
his rueful look the flare of anger
that struck the match

nothing we'd planned to happen did
we have all been saved so many times

why I should think of this
years later in such elegant air
not wondering what happened to him
or feeling regret but thinking instead
how the signs on abandoned motels
west of Langtry Texas have faded more
each year

EXCELLENT BEDS
just a pale red whisper now
TILE BATHROOMS
ghost of a promise
receding into stucco wall
SLEEP WELL HERE

*

LULLABY FOR REGRET

I'll tuck you in, thin sliver
that needles my wake.
I'll stroke your little loose suitcase,
your clanging spur.

Who were you looking for
all this time? That other girl
never grew up, that perfect one.
Only the bumbler survived.

Waking in Scranton
in the old train station,
I felt quicksand
creep up my legs.
It was you, and I had to host you
for two whole days.

I felt you in Pittsburgh,
Portland, and Honolulu,
pinned to the sky's big silence
with my six intoxicating leis.

So, stop.
Here's the pillowcase studded with
punctuation.
Here's the song about the woods
and the fields.
It's hard to feel regret
where the air's so big
all the days we haven't lived yet

breathe in and out
their grand extravagance
and we could stay there
and nothing would go wrong.

*

NEXT TIME

Gingko trees live 1,000 years.
Eating the leaves will clear your brain.
When I heard about them, I thought of my mother,
how much I would like to sit under one with her
in the ancient shade, nibbling
the flesh, the stem, the central vein.

*

LOVE LETTER, HATE LETTER

Sometimes a whole world spills
onto the table, with its own ragged trees,
crooked gutters, the small dog who whimpers
at night. I circle it carefully
but the world feels complete.
Even the clay Maria with her baskets
of clay fruit would be easier to
communicate with, even a spoon.

Once in an airport I stared for thirty minutes
at a man wearing sharp green shoes exactly matching
his suit and lopsided tie. How long had he searched
to find them? Later it seemed foolish
to feel so moved, to make up stories for
a man who wanted to be green.
Perhaps it had nothing to do with shoes,
rather the nervous fluttering of his hand
as he scanned a paper, or the sense that
no one waited anywhere to pick him up.

I find I am hated and loved
for the same things—what I couldn't do.
Once I mailed angry letters to newspapers
and once, to a king. I can't remember why.
Shadows behind us change shape
in their own light. How innocent we are!
Some days we only accept mail for strangers.
I envy the post office, its wonderful lines:
No such person at this address.

*

BRUSHING LIVES

In Alexandria a waitress skimmed between tables
in a black sheath skirt, her jaw precise and elegant,
hair waving out from a definite scalp like 1942—
I saw the most beautiful woman of my life that day.
She held herself brilliantly, one gracious arm
balancing a stumpy Coke bottle on a tray.
Said "yes" and "thank you" in a deep, dazed voice.
And the men went on talking. And the cars outside
were not headed toward her door.

Later my father appeared with a husky voice.
In a shop so dark he had to blink twice
an ancient man sunk low on a stool said,
"You talk like the men who lived in the world
when I was young." Wouldn't say more,
till my father mentioned Palestine
and the gentleman rose, both arms out, streaming
cheeks. "I have stopped saying it. So many years."
My father held him there, held Palestine, in the dark,
at the corner of two honking streets.
He got lost coming back to our hotel.

Who else? They're out there.
The ones who could save or break us,
the ones we're lonely for,
the ones with an answer the size of a
pocket handkerchief or a shovel,
the ones who know the story before
our own story starts,
the ones who suffered what we most fear
and survived.

Sometimes we stand side-by-side
on the platform waiting for the train
and the miracle is not the meeting
but the miss—
we feel full already, we have enough friends.

*

MORNING PAPER, SOCIETY PAGE

I can never see fashion models,
lean angular cheeks, strutting hips
and blooming hair, without thinking of
the skulls at the catacombs in Lima, Peru.
How we climbed down from blurred markets
to find a thousand unnamed friends smiling at us
as if they too could advertise
a coming style.

*

EVEN AT WAR

Loose in his lap, the hands.
And always a necktie,
as some worlds are made complete
by single things.
Graveled voice,
bucket raised on old ropes.
You know how a man can get up,
get dressed, and think
the world is waiting for him?
At night darkness knits
a giant cap to hold the dreams in.
A wardrobe of neckties with slanted stripes.
Outside oranges are sleeping, eggplants,
fields of wild sage. An order
from the government said,
You will no longer pick this sage
that flavors your whole life.
And all the hands smiled.
Tonight the breathing air carries
headlines that will cross the ocean
by tomorrow. Bar the door.

*

THE GRIEVING RING

When word of his death arrived
we sat in a circle for days
crying or not crying

long ago in the other country
girls balanced buckets
on their heads

now the old sweet water
rose from the spring
to swallow us

brothers shrank
children grew old
it felt fine to say nothing
about him
or something small

the way he carried
oranges and falafel
in his pockets

the way he was always
slightly mad

what he said to each
the last time
we saw him
hurt the worst

those unwritten letters
banging each head
till it felt bruised

now he would stand at the mirror
knotting his tie
for the rest of so many lives

*

FOR THE 500TH DEAD PALESTINIAN, IBTISAM BOZIEH

Little sister Ibtisam,
our sleep flounders, our sleep tugs
the cord of your name.
Dead at 13, for staring through
the window into a gun barrel
which did not know you wanted to be
a doctor.

I would smooth your life in my hands,
pull you back. Had I stayed in your land,
I might have been dead too,
for something simple like staring
or shouting what was true
and getting kicked out of school.
I wandered stony afternoons
owning all their vastness.

Now I would give them to you,
guiltily, you, not me.
Throwing this ragged grief into the street,
scissoring news stories free from the page
but they live on my desk with letters, not cries.

How do we carry the endless surprise
of all our deaths? Becoming doctors
for one another, Arab, Jew,
instead of guarding tumors of pain
as if they hold us upright?

People in other countries speak easily
of being early, late.
Some will live to be eighty.
Some who never saw it
will not forget your face.

*

THOSE WHOM WE DO NOT KNOW

To feel the love of people whom we love is a fire that
feeds our life. But to feel the affection that comes from
those whom we do not know . . . is something still greater
and more beautiful . . .
—Pablo Neruda

I.

Because our country has entered
into war, we can have
no pleasant pauses anymore—

instead, the nervous turning
one side to another,
each corner crowded by the far
but utterly particular
voices of the dead,

of trees, fish, children,
calling, calling,
wearing the colorful plastic shoes
so beloved in the Middle East,
bleeding from the skull,
the sweet hollow along the neck.

I forget why. It's been changed.
For whatever it was
we will crush the vendor
who stacked sesame rings
on a tray
inside the steady gaze
of stones.
He will lose his balance
after years of perfect balance.

Catch him! Inside every sleep
he keeps falling.

2.

I support all people on earth
who have bodies like and unlike my body,
skins and moles and old scars,
secret and public hair,
crooked toes. I support
those who have done nothing large,
sifter of lentils, sifter of wisdoms,
speak. If we have killed no one
in the name of anything bad or good,
may light feed our leafiest veins.

I support clothes in the wash-kettle,
a woman stirring and stirring
with stick, paddle, soaking out grime,
simple clothes the size of bodies
pinned to the sky.

3.

What we learned left us.
None of it held.

Now the words ignite.
Slogans knot around necks
till faces bulge.

Windows of sand, doorways,
sense of shifting
each time you blink—

that dune? Used to be
a house. And the desert
soaking up echoes—

those whom we did not know
think they know us now.

INSIDE THE RIDDLE

It's blue in here.

There are grocery stores, with soap.

I'm looking for someone
who might have an answer
big enough not to be insulting,
but everyone looks preoccupied,
blankly solemn.

I'm staring at an umbrella,
a yard shrine on El Paso Street.
What is it keeping away?
Vagrant dogs, dogs with shark's teeth,
men with anchors blurred
beneath their sleeves.

This little house of Mary,
this concrete grotto studded
with seashells or chipped glass,
I would like to be a Catholic
with such a straight faith.

Or a Muslim, fasting and praying—
I would kneel on stones
beside the men of Cairo.

To believe God has reasons
seems too petty for God.

*

SHOULDERS

A man crosses the street in rain,
stepping gently, looking two times north and south,
because his son is asleep on his shoulder.

No car must splash him.
No car drive too near to his shadow.

This man carries the world's most sensitive cargo
but he's not marked.
Nowhere does his jacket say FRAGILE,
HANDLE WITH CARE.

His ear fills up with breathing.
He hears the hum of a boy's dream
deep inside him.

We're not going to be able
to live in this world
if we're not willing to do what he's doing
with one another.

The road will only be wide.
The rain will never stop falling.

*

ACKNOWLEDGEMENTS AND DEDICATIONS

Grateful acknowledgement is made to the editors of the following journals in which some of these poems (or earlier versions of them) first appeared: *Chaminade Literary Review, The Cream City Review, The Georgia Review, Green Mountains Review, Kaimana/ Literary Arts Hawaii, Hayden's Ferry Review, New Virginia Review, Northern Lights, Paintbrush, Poets of the Lake, Our Own Clues: Poets of the Lake 2, Southwestern American Literature, Sycamore Review, Visions International, Wilderness.*

"What Brings Us Out" appeared in *New American Poets of the '90's,* edited by Jack Myers and Roger Weingarten, David R. Godine, 1991.

"What Brings Us Out, "Swimmer, Blessed Sea," "Even at War" and "Saved" appeared in *Texas Poets in Concert/A Quartet,* University of North Texas Press, 1990.

"Valentine for Ernest Mann" appeared in *The Place My Words Are Looking For,* edited by Paul Janeczko, (Bradbury Press/ Macmillan, 1990) and in *Imagine Poetry Magazine,* from Multi Source, Prentice Hall, Canada, 1993.

"From Here to There," appeared in a chapbook, *Invisible,* Trilobite Press, Denton, Texas, 1987.

"Problems with the Story" appeared in *What Will Suffice: Contemporary American Poets on the Art of Poetry* edited by Christopher Merrill (Gibbs M. Smith, 1994).

"Swimmer, Blessed Sea" appeared as a handmade broadside by Beck and Chuck Whitehead, Southwest Craft Center, San Antonio.

A number of poems appeared in a chapbook from Wings Press, Houston, 1993.

The excerpt from the poem "No Place to Hide," by Tommy Olofsson from *Elemental Poems,* copyright © 1991, by White

ABOUT THE AUTHOR

Naomi Shihab Nye's poems and stories have appeared in numerous textbooks and anthologies. Her collections of poems include *Different Ways to Pray*, *Hugging the Jukebox* (the National Poetry Series and an ALA Notable Book), and *Yellow Glove*. In 1994, *Words Under the Words: Selected Poems* will appear from Far Corner Books and Eighth Mountain Press in Oregon. Her children's picture book *Sitti's Secrets* appeared spring 1994 from Four Winds Press/Macmillan, which also published her award-winning collection of poems from around the world, *This Same Sky*, in 1992. She has received three Pushcart Prizes, two Texas Institute of Letters Poetry Prizes, the Charity Randall Prize for Spoken Poetry from the International Poetry Forum, and the I. B. Lavan Award from the Academy of American Poets. She has traveled abroad on three USIA-sponsored Arts America speaking tours throughout the Middle East and Asia. Also a songwriter and singer, she lives with her husband, photographer Michael Nye and son, Madison, in San Antonio, Texas.

BOA Editions, Ltd.
American Poets Continuum Series

Vol. 1   *The Führer Bunker: A Cycle of Poems in Progress*
W. D. Snodgrass

Vol. 2   *She*
M.L. Rosenthal

Vol. 3   *Living With Distance*
Ralph J. Mills, Jr.

Vol. 4   *Not Just Any Death*
Michael Waters

Vol. 5   *That Was Then: New and Selected Poems*
Isabella Gardner

Vol. 6   *Things That Happen Where There Aren't Any People*
William Stafford

Vol. 7   *The Bridge of Change: Poems 1974–1980*
John Logan

Vol. 8   *Signatures*
Joseph Stroud

Vol. 9   *People Live Here: Selected Poems 1949–1983*
Louis Simpson

Vol. 10 *Yin*
Carolyn Kizer

Vol. 11 *Duhamel: Ideas of Order in Little Canada*
Bill Tremblay

Vol. 12 *Seeing It Was So*
Anthony Piccione

Vol. 13 *Hyam Plutzik: The Collected Poems*

Vol. 14 *Good Woman: Poems and a Memoir 1969–1980*
Lucille Clifton

Vol. 15 *Next: New Poems*
Lucille Clifton

Vol. 16 *Roxa: Voices of the Culver Family*
William B. Patrick

Vol. 17 *John Logan: The Collected Poems*

Vol. 18 *Isabella Gardner: The Collected Poems*

Vol. 19 *The Sunken Lightship*
Peter Makuck

Vol. 20 *The City in Which I Love You*
Li-Young Lee

Vol. 21 *Quilting: Poems 1987–1990*
Lucille Clifton

Vol. 22 *John Logan: The Collected Fiction*

Vol. 23 *Shenandoah and Other Verse Plays*
Delmore Schwartz